Ideal Couple

By
Shaykh Mufti Saiful Islām

JKN Publications

© Copyright by JKN Publications

First Published in October 2017
ISBN: 978-1909114-27-2

British Library Cataloguing in Publication Data
A catalogue record for this book is available from the British Library.

All Rights Reserved. No part of this book may be reproduced, stored in a retrieval system or transmitted in any form or by any means, electronic, mechanical, photocopying, recording or otherwise, without the prior permission of the copyright owner.

Publisher's Note:

Every care and attention has been put into the production of this book. If however, you find any errors they are our own, for which we seek Allāh's ﷻ forgiveness and reader's pardon.

Published by:

JKN Publications
118 Manningham Lane
Bradford
West Yorkshire
BD8 7JF
United Kingdom

t: +44 (0) 1274 308 456 | w: www.jkn.org.uk | e: info@jkn.org.uk

Book Title: Ideal Couple

Author: Shaykh Mufti Saiful Islām

Printed by Mega Printing in Turkey

"In the Name of Allāh, the Most Beneficent, the Most Merciful"

Contents

Introduction… … … … … … … … … … … … … … … …	6
The Importance and Virtues of Marriage............................	8
Twenty Five Awesome Tips for a Beautiful Life!..................	12
Amazing Du'ā of Rasūlullāh ﷺ……………………………	14
Imām Ahmad's ﷺ Ten Golden Advice to his Son Before his Wedding Day..	16
Advice to my "ONLINE" Daughter.com… … … … … … …	19
A Happy Couple...	28
How to Make Amends after a Domestic Dispute … … … ….	30
Finding the Right Person to Marry… … … … … … … … …	31
Cooking Tips… … … … … … … … … … … … … … … ….	36
"Who Is a Man"… … … … … … … … … … … … … … …	38
The Two Farewells of a Woman… … … … … … … … … …	40
Just a Muslimah… … … … … … … … … … … … … … ….	43
I Love My Husband… … … … … … … … … … … … … …	44
The Status of a Woman… … … … … … … … … … … … …	47
A Bride's Death in Sujūd… … … … … … … … … … … … …	49
The Shaykh and the General… … … … … … … … … … …	52
Not for Sale for Every Male… … … … … … … … … … … …	53
An Ideal Marriage… … … … … … … … … … … … … … …	55
Tasbīhāt of Sayyidah Fātimah ﷺ……………………………	56
Recipe for a Happy Marriage… … … … … … … … … … …	58

Nikāh..	61
She Broke the Internet!...	63
The Etiquettes of Conversing with One's Husband……………..	67
Ten Points to maintain a Happy Marriage… ……..……………..	70
Live Happily… … … … …….… … … … … … … … … … … …..	73
A Couple's Conversation… … … … … … … …..… … … … ……..	75
Rules for a Happy Marriage… … … … … … … … … … … … ….....	77

Introduction

All Praises are due to Allāh ﷻ, the Lord of the Universe. May Peace and Salutations be upon His final Messenger, Muhammad ﷺ, his family, his Noble Companions ﷺ and all those who follow their righteous lifestyles until the Last Day.

Allāh ﷻ has allowed men and women to share intimate companionship with each other through the contract of 'marriage'. Marriage withstands a high level of importance in Islām, given that it is a major Sunnah of all the Prophets including our beloved Messenger ﷺ. As well as fulfilling the basic nature of man and woman's sexual desires in a lawful manner, marriage also provides a bond of companionship and love for the sake of Allāh ﷻ. This bond is such that it allows both to share emotional support to one another.

In spite of this, one must appreciate that marriage is accompanied with many responsibilities which many couples unfortunately overlook. Every couple must ensure that they thoroughly understand every aspect related to marriage with an open mind and heart, mirrored by the notable examples of our beloved Messenger ﷺ and our pious predecessors.

We should learn from our predecessor's examples and try to emulate their mannerisms and behaviour so to induce happiness in our marriages. This will control or even eliminate the increased number of divorces, marital stress and disputes.

This book is a compilation of inspiring stories and articles which contain useful tips and life skills for a husband and wife to develop to enhance their affection for one another and maintain a harmonious marriage. It is hoped that this book will prove beneficial for all of our readers who are struggling with their relationship.

May Allāh ﷻ accept this compilation and enable this book to be beneficial for all couples. May Allāh ﷻ reward Shaykh Mufti Saiful Islām Sāhib immensely for facilitating this project of compilation and his efforts. Āmīn!

Palwasha Ustrana
Student of Jāmiah Khātamun Nabiyeen (Rotherham)
October 2017/Muharram 1439

The Importance and Virtues of Marriage

Marriage is a great blessing from Allāh ﷻ. Once married, they are permitted to derive pleasure from one another and relatively, become life partners and share each other's happiness, pleasure, joy and sorrow. There are many Dīni (religious) and worldly benefits in marriage if all Shar'ee requirements are met.

Marriage transpires a unique affection and bond between the husband and wife. Allāh ﷻ states in the Holy Qur'ān;

وَمِنْ اٰيٰتِهٖ اَنْ خَلَقَ لَكُمْ مِّنْ اَنْفُسِكُمْ اَزْوَاجًا لِّتَسْكُنُوْٓا اِلَيْهَا وَجَعَلَ بَيْنَكُمْ مَّوَدَّةً وَّرَحْمَةً

"And it is amongst His signs that He has created for you from amongst yourselves wives so that you may find tranquillity in them and He has established love and mercy between you"
(30: 21)

Sayyidunā Abdullāh Ibn Abbās ؓ relates that the Holy Prophet ﷺ said, "You shall not find an example of any two mutual lovers that is equal to marriage." (Mishkāt)

Some Ahādīth related to the importance and virtues of marriage are mentioned below.

1. Sayyidunā Anas Ibn Mālik ؓ relates that once, three Companions came to the house of (one of) the wives of the Holy Prophet ﷺ in-

quiring about the worship performed by the Holy Prophet ﷺ. When they were informed it seemed insufficient to them. They said, "Where are we (in comparison) to the Holy Prophet ﷺ as Allāh ﷻ has forgiven all his past and future sins." So one of them asserted, "As for me I am going to perform Salāh throughout the night permanently (without retiring to bed)." The second Companion asserted, "I am going to fast throughout the year and will not miss a single fast."

The third Companion said, "I will disassociate myself from women and will never marry." The Holy Prophet ﷺ (after being informed) approached them and asked, "Are you the ones who said such and such things? By Allāh ﷻ, I am the most fearful of Allāh ﷻ and the most pious towards Him however, I fast and break my fast, I perform Salāh (at night) and sleep and I also marry women, so whomsoever diverts from my Sunnah is not from amongst me." (Bukhāri)

2. Marriage is a means of repelling many illicit acts, for instance fornication, casting unlawful glances and adultery. The Holy Prophet ﷺ said, "O group of youth! Whosoever amongst you has (adequate) means of marrying then he ought to do so, because it lowers the gaze and protects the chastity. But whosoever does not have the ability should fast for indeed it would serve as a protection for him."

(Bukhāri)

3. The Holy Prophet ﷺ is also reported to have said, "The entire world is a place of commodity and the best commodity (that one can have) is a pious wife." (Muslim)

4. Marriage was not merely the Sunnah of the Holy Prophet ﷺ but also the Sunnah of all the Prophets ﷺ. It is related in Tirmizi by Sayyidunā Abū Ayyūb Al-Ansāri ؓ that the Holy Prophet ﷺ said, "Four matters are from amongst the Sunnats of all the Prophets ﷺ:

a) To have Hayā (modesty and bashfulness).
b) To apply Itr (fragrance).
c) To use Miswāk (tooth-stick).
d) To perform marriage."

5. Marriage completes half of one's faith. Sayyidunā Anas Ibn Mālik ؓ relates that the Holy Prophet ﷺ said, "When a person marries then he fulfils half of his faith, therefore he should fear Allāh ﷻ (for the completion) of the remaining half." (Mishkāt).

Completion of one's half of faith refer to instilling many good qualities, e.g. prevention from fornication and adultery, prevention from evil gazes, striving to become an ideal husband or wife, fulfilling each other's rights, striving to become an ideal father or mother, maturity, wisdom, God consciousness, practicing patience and fear of Allāh ﷻ (when carrying out one's responsibility) etc.

As well as forming a union and a social institution between a man and a woman, marriage is also an act of continuous Ibādah (worship). Other forms of worship such as Salāh, Fasting, Hajj etc, although being amongst the greatest forms of worship, are restricted by time and place. Marriage on the other hand is not restricted but its worship takes into effect instantly after the solemnization of the wedlock. But this is only when all the correct guidelines of Islām are followed.

The Holy Prophet ﷺ is reported to have said, "Fulfil your desires (in a Halāl way) as this is also Sadaqah (charity)." Upon this, the Sahābah ؓ inquired, "How can this be a Sadaqah? If a person is fulfilling his desires then why should he be entitled to reward?" The Holy Prophet ﷺ replied, "If a human being fulfils his desires in a Harām way he will be sinful, similarly if someone fulfils his desires through Halāl measures then he receives reward." (Muslim)

To provide expenses for one's family is an act of Sadaqah. The Holy Prophet ﷺ is reported to have said, "Whenever a Muslim spends upon his family (whatever amount) with the aspiration of earning Thawāb (reward) then for him (this is) Sadaqah." (Muslim)

Twenty Five Awesome Tips for a Beautiful Life!

1. Take a 10-30 minute walk every day and while you walk, SMILE. It is the ultimate antidepressant.

2. Sit in silence for at least 10 minutes each day.

3. When you wake up in the morning, pray and ask the Almighty's guidance for your purpose.

4. Eat more foods that grow on trees and plants and eat less of those that are processed.

5. Drink green tea and plenty of water. Eat blueberries, broccoli and almonds.

6. Try to make at least three people smile each day.

7. Don't waste your precious energy on gossip, issues of the past, negative thoughts or things you cannot control. Instead, invest your energy in positive thinking.

8. Consume a nutritious breakfast, a healthy meal during lunch and a light supper.

9. Life is good if you are optimistic.

10. Life is too short to waste time hating others. Forgive them for everything!

11. Don't take yourself so seriously. No one else does.

12. You don't have to win every argument. Agree to disagree and try to win the hearts of people.

13. Make peace with your past so it won't spoil the present.

14. Don't compare your life to others. You have no idea what their journey is all about.

15. No one is in charge of your happiness except you.

16. Frame every so-called disaster with these words: 'In five years, will this matter?'

17. Help the needy, be generous! Be a 'Giver' not a 'Taker.'

18. What other people think of you should never concern you.

19. Time heals everything.

20. However good or bad a situation is, it will change.

21. Your job won't take care of you when you are sick. Your friends will. Stay in touch with them.

22. Envy is a waste of time. You already have all you need.

23. Each night before you go to bed, pray to Allāh ﷻ and be thankful for what you've accomplished today!

24. Remember that you are too blessed to be stressed.

25. Share this knowledge to everyone you know to help them lead a happy life!

Amazing Du'ā of Rasūlullāh ﷺ

A senior Ālim from the UK relates:

On a recent trip to Sahāranpūr, we were fortunate to meet Shaykh Āqil Sāhib, a great Muhaddith of India, and the son in law of Shaykhul Hadīth, Maulāna Muhammad Zakariyya Kandhālwi ﷺ. Whilst sitting with him, he taught us this beautiful Du'ā and mentioned to us that Allāh ﷻ has put great effect in it. People who are not getting along very well with friends and relatives, couples who are fighting and arguing regularly should read this Du'ā in abundance.

He mentioned that one particular Ālim fell into some family feuds and as a result started suffering much worry and grief. After reciting this Du'ā several times, he was relieved from his grief.

The respected Shaykh also mentioned that once he was in Madīnah Munawwarah and a woman met his family in the Haram Sharīf at the time of Maghrib. She complained about her relationship with her husband saying that he was very cold towards her on this journey and was not speaking to her at all. Shaykh's respected family taught her this Du'ā and encouraged her to recite it regularly.

The next morning at the time of Fajr, when she met her, this woman could not stop thanking her for teaching her the Du'ā. Her husband's mood suddenly changed and he has become much warmer towards her than before.

Recitation of the following Du'ā abundantly will unite the hearts, Inshā-Allāh.

اَللّٰهُمَّ اَلِّفْ بَيْنَ قُلُوْبِنَا، وَأَصْلِحْ ذَاتَ بَيْنِنَا، وَاهْدِنَا سُبُلَ السَّلَامِ، وَنَجِّنَا مِنَ الظُّلُمَاتِ إِلَى النُّوْرِ وَجَنِّبْنَا الْفَوَاحِشَ مَا ظَهَرَ مِنْهَا وَمَا بَطَنَ وَبَارِكْ لَنَا فِيْ أَسْمَاعِنَا، وَأَبْصَارِنَا وَقُلُوْبِنَا، وَأَزْوَاجِنَا، وَذُرِّيَّاتِنَا وَتُبْ عَلَيْنَآ إِنَّكَ أَنْتَ التَّوَّابُ الرَّحِيْمُ

O' Allāh! Place affection between our hearts, rectify matters between ourselves, guide us to the ways of peace, safeguard us from darkness towards light, spare us from (all kinds of) indecency which are apparent as well as those that are hidden, bless us in our hearing, our seeing, our hearts, our spouses and our children and forgive us, indeed You are the One Who greatly accepts repentance, One Who is Merciful.

Imām Ahmad's ﷺ Ten Golden Advice to his Son Before his Wedding Day

Dear son! you will not attain happiness in your home except by ten characteristics which you must show to your wife. So remember them and be enthusiastic in acting upon them.

1&2. As for the first two; women like attention and they like to be told clearly that they are loved. So don't be stingy in expressing your love for your wife. If you become limited in expressing your love, you will create a barrier of harshness between you and her in which case there will be a decrease in affection.

3. Ladies hate a strict and (a constant) over cautious man. So use each quality appropriately. This will be more appealing to love and will bring you peace of mind.

4. Women like from their husbands what their husbands like from them, i.e. kind words, good looks, clean clothes and a pleasant odour. Therefore, always appear well-groomed in front of them.

5. The woman is the queen of her home. As long as she remains in it, she feels that she is sitting on her throne and the queen of the house. Abstain from disrupting this palace of hers and never attempt to dethrone her, otherwise you will be viewed as snatching her sovereignty from her.

6. A woman wants to love her husband but at the same time does not want to lose her family. So do not put yourself and her family on the same scale, otherwise her choice will be down to either you or her family. Even if she chooses you over her family, she will still remain in anxiety which will eventually turn into hatred towards you.

7. Surely every woman has been created from a curved rib which is the secret of her beauty and attraction. This is no defect in her, because 'the eyebrows look beautiful when they are curved'. So if she errs, do not rebuke her in a manner in which there is no gentleness. Don't attempt to straighten her otherwise you will break her and her breaking, is divorcing her. At the same time correct her mistakes, otherwise her crookedness will increase and she will become arrogant with her ego. Thereafter, she will never soften for you and she won't listen to you, so stay in between the two.

8. It is in the women's nature to be ungrateful towards their husbands and to deny favours every so often. If you were to be nice to her for her whole life but you grieved her once, she will say, "I have never seen any good from you". So don't let this make you dislike her or to run away from her. If you dislike this feature of hers, you will be pleased with many of her other good habits, so set a balance.

9. There are times when a woman undergoes physical weaknesses and fatigue of the mind. Those are the occasions when Allāh ﷻ has relieved her from compulsory worships and postponed the days of fasting for her. During these days, treat her with utmost kindness.

Just as Allāh ﷻ has relieved her of the duties, you too should lessen your demands and instructions from her.

10. Last but not least, "know that a woman is like a captive with you. Therefore, have mercy upon her."

Advice to my "ONLINE" Daughter.com

It seems like yesterday when you were taking your first few steps and trying to walk. You tried to stand and then fell down with a thump so many times but you kept trying and eventually you took your first step. Alhamdulillāh, I was proud of you then and I am proud of you now.

My daughter, you have all grown up but the challenges you faced when you were learning to walk and even now they remain. Their nature may have changed but their severity have not. Yesterday, when you fell on your back while trying to stand, was not anything major but yet, you managed to stand up again. Today, when you fall on your back, it may not be so easy for you to get up and walk again because the injuries may be to your soul and to your Īmān, so watch out!

My daughter, I bought you a phone and laptop for your personal use because I trust you for using them responsibly and that Allāh ﷻ will guide you in your decisions when doing so. I still fear Shaytān's meddling and also fear for your innocence. You will forever be "my little daughter" and nothing will change that. No matter how many times I am told how you are all grown up now, as your father, I will always be protective and look out for you. I cannot help it, so forgive the silliness of this old man! I love you and I care dearly about you. I was there when you were born, I called the Adhān in your ear and I took you home on your first day, so I cannot help it. By Allāh! I cannot help but to look out for you!

We may have some differences of opinion and Allāh ﷻ has given you the right to exercise your own opinion. Despite our disagreements, I will NEVER stand in your way but I would want you to go about making decisions in the right way.

Shūra (Consultation)

My daughter, you have the right to make your own decision but if they are based on the commandments of Allāh ﷻ and the Noble Sunnah of the Holy Prophet ﷺ, then the blessings of Allāh ﷻ will be part of your decision and they will enrich your life. Allāh ﷻ says in the Holy Qur'ān,

$$\text{وَالَّذِيْنَ اسْتَجَابُوْا لِرَبِّهِمْ وَأَقَامُوا الصَّلَاةَ وَأَمْرُهُمْ شُوْرَىٰ بَيْنَهُمْ وَمِمَّا رَزَقْنَاهُمْ يُنْفِقُوْنَ}$$

"And those who have responded to their Lord (in submission to Him), and have established Salāh, and whose affairs are (settled) with mutual consultation between them, and who spend out of what We have given to them." (42:38)

However, you must consult with the right people! My daughter, Allāh ﷻ has commanded us to refer our matters to scholars. Allāh ﷻ says in the Holy Qur'ān,

$$\text{فَاسْأَلُوا أَهْلَ الذِّكْرِ إِنْ كُنْتُمْ لَا تَعْلَمُونَ}$$

"So, ask the people (having the knowledge) of the Reminder (the earlier scriptures), if you do not know." (16:43)

You have trusted your father for so long and it is most appreciated, but now you must think for yourself in order to progress in your Dunyā and Hereafter. I will not be around forever and I advise you to ascertain the credibility of the scholars whom you consult. Not everyone who is active on an Islamic forum, or has millions of followers on Facebook, or appears persuasive on YouTube, can be trusted. Not everyone who can write eloquently or speak fluently is trustworthy.

This Dīn of Allāh ﷻ was revealed upon the Holy Prophet ﷺ through the noble and trusted Sayyidunā Jibrīl عليه السلام, then it was transmitted to the Sahābah ﷺ and so on until it has reached us. We have ensured that we have acquired it from noble scholars, men and women of trustworthiness and Taqwa, who were (and are) trusted with their nobility and credibility. Facebook, Twitter, YouTube, WhatsApp and Islamic forums do not change the rules of seeking Dīn.

Sacred knowledge was in the hearts of men, then it moved into books but the keys to these books are in the hands of scholars. This implies the necessity of acquiring knowledge from the people who master it.

My daughter, know that authentic knowledge will be taken away by the passing of sincere scholars and that misguided fools will take their places. These fools will be utterly misguided and they will misguide others.

Allāh ﷻ does not remove sacred knowledge by mere extraction from the servants hearts rather, by taking back the souls of Islamic scholars until, He has not left a single scholar. People will take the ignorant as leaders, who will be asked for legal opinion and they will issue them without knowledge. Thus they are misguided and misguiding. (Bukhāri)

The second unshaken component of decision making is Istikhārah, as suggested by the Holy Prophet ﷺ. Many are mistaken in thinking that Istikhārah is only for marriage. Know that it is for every need in your life, no matter how small the need may be. Those who beseech their Lord and ask for guidance are guided but those that are the haughty, who rely on their intellect and experience, miss out. My daughter, do not be from the arrogant and the haughty because these are the traits of Shaytān.

Istikhārah should be done regardless of the feelings about a decision. If you feel strongly about a decision and secure in it, then this feeling will be strengthened and the matter will be made easy for you. If nothing comes to your mind on the first day and the anxiety and indecisiveness continues, you should repeat it the next day and so on for a week. By the grace of Allāh ﷻ you will come to know the good or evil of the matter. It is not necessary for you to have dreams about the issue.

Marriage without a Walī

Now, let us talk about the issues pertaining to your friend, Fātimah, who you briefly talked about this morning. You said that Fātimah met someone on Facebook whom she intends to marry and she believes that her father's objections to her choice are against Sharī'ah. You also said that Fātimah believes that, since she is Hanafī, she can go ahead and get married without a Walī.

I remember little Fātimah from Madrasah days, a likeable little girl who always considered her words before speaking. In this case, however, I think she may be getting a little ahead of herself and here is why:

Marriage without a Walī according to Imām Mālik ﷺ, Imām Shāfi'ī ﷺ and Imām Ahmad ﷺ and their three Madhāhib is invalid. Marriage without a Walī according to Imām Abū Yūsuf ﷺ, Imām Muhammad ﷺ in the Hanafī Madhab is also invalid.

Marriage of a mature woman (Bāligha) without a Walī, according to Imām Abū Hanīfah ﷺ is valid, although the Sunnah is to involve the Walī.

A number of Hanafī Ulamā have given Fatwa upon the illustrious opinion of the students of Imām Abū Hanīfah ﷺ and regard marriage without a Walī as invalid. On the other hand, there are Ulamā who regard marriage without a Walī as valid. Nevertheless, they clearly discourage and advise against it.

Furthermore, if Fātimah is choosing to take the dispensation within the Hanafī Madhab then she should also realize that the Hanafī Madhab has strict recommendations for compatibility (Kafā'at) in marriage and an Islamic Sharī'ah council can rule in favour of her father and annul the marriage due to incompatibility.

In other words, Fātimah cannot take dispensation from the Hanafī Madhab on marriage without a Walī, but then ignore rulings pertaining to compatibility (Kafā'at).

I do not know why Fātimah's father disagrees with her choice. Regardless, I do not understand why Fātimah thinks her father's reasons are invalid, while hers are valid. To me, she should seek an independent opinion; she should remove herself and her father from the equation and discuss the issue with an Islamic Sharī'ah Council. If they deliberate and then rule that her father's reasons are invalid, then she can let a Mufti act as a Walī on her behalf. The noble Sunnah of the Holy Prophet ﷺ has given us guidance in this matter:

"If they dispute, then the ruler is the guardian of the one who has no guardian." (Tirmizi, Abū Dāwūd)

Clearly, there is a dispute between Fātimah and her father. However, instead of relying on her judgment and stripping her marriage of the blessings of Allāh ﷻ, she should contact her nearest Islamic Shari'ah council since we do not have any Muslim rulers. That way, not only will her decision be independently verified, but her interests and wishes will be protected as well.

Finally, Fātimah should realize that Allāh ﷻ has stipulated the condition of a Walī for Muslim women for a reason and she should reconsider breaking away from the protection He has given her through her Walī. While she has the right to marry the person of her choice, she should go about it the right way - ensuring the pleasure and blessings of Allāh ﷻ

Seeking Separation from Marriage
You seem to be affected by the situation of Khadījah on Facebook and the hardship which she is enduring. My daughter, first and foremost adhere to the advice of Shaykh Ashraf Alī Thānwi ﷺ who said,

"If a person comes to you with one of his eyeballs in his hand claiming that so and so has done it. Do not believe it until you hear the other side of the story because it could be that he removed the eye of the other person and in retaliation, he punched and removed his eye and now he has come to you with a complaint!"

I fully understand the plight of Khadījah as what she has written has affected you. So make Du'ā for her, console her and comfort her but neither judge her, nor issue a judgment. It is easy for someone to create an ID online and post a story. You are neither in a position to verify nor arbitrate it and if you decide to favour one party over another, based on reading a Facebook wall or a post online, then know that you have been emotionally affected. Detach yourself (emotionally) so you can retain your thinking and give the best advice.

The solution is to refer Khadījah to local scholars or to an Islamic Sharī'ah Council and let them advise accordingly.

My daughter! No new Dīn will come and no new guidance will be revealed just because I have bought you a new phone and a laptop. The principles of Islamic Sharī'ah remain the same.

Don't trust everything you read on the internet!
Don't trust everyone who claims to be a Shaykh on the internet!

Learn to trust and refer your matters to the scholars whom you can verify and whom others have relied on their judgement.

The difference between instant internet celebrities and real scholars can be beautifully understood from these verses of the Holy Qur'ān.

أَلَمْ تَرَ كَيْفَ ضَرَبَ اللّٰهُ مَثَلًا كَلِمَةً طَيِّبَةً كَشَجَرَةٍ طَيِّبَةٍ أَصْلُهَا ثَابِتٌ وَفَرْعُهَا فِي السَّمَآءِ

"Have you not seen how Allāh has set forth a parable of a good word that is like a good tree, having its root firm and its branches in the sky." (14:24)

تُؤْتِي أُكُلَهَا كُلَّ حِينٍ بِإِذْنِ رَبِّهَا ۗ وَيَضْرِبُ اللّٰهُ الْأَمْثَالَ لِلنَّاسِ لَعَلَّهُمْ يَتَذَكَّرُونَ

"It brings its fruits at all times with the Will of its Lord. Allāh sets forth the parables for the people, so that they may take lesson." (14:25)

$$\text{وَمَثَلُ كَلِمَةٍ خَبِيثَةٍ كَشَجَرَةٍ خَبِيثَةٍ اجْتُثَّتْ مِن فَوْقِ الْأَرْضِ مَا لَهَا مِن قَرَارٍ}$$

"And the parable of a bad word is like a bad tree, removed from the top of the soil, having no firm root." [14:26]

The 24/7 switched on world of the internet and Tweets of the unknown cannot be compared to the sincere efforts of those scholars who sacrificed everything to teach us our religion. Your father always considered it a source of pride to sit at the feet of the scholars to gain his Islām and I strongly advise you to do the same.

There is nothing that I have seen in the past few decades before and after your birth, which has convinced me to change my mind. However, I have witnessed hundreds of sensational speakers and writers come and go! Adopt and adhere to Taqwa because it will save you and deliver you from all your problems:

$$\text{وَمَن يَتَّقِ اللَّهَ يَجْعَل لَّهُ مَخْرَجًا وَيَرْزُقْهُ مِنْ حَيْثُ لَا يَحْتَسِبُ وَمَن يَتَوَكَّلْ عَلَى اللَّهِ فَهُوَ حَسْبُهُ إِنَّ اللَّهَ بَالِغُ أَمْرِهِ قَدْ جَعَلَ اللَّهُ لِكُلِّ شَيْءٍ قَدْرًا}$$

"Whoever fears Allāh, He brings forth a way out for him and provides him (with what he needs) from where he does not even imagine. And whoever places his trust in Allāh, He is sufficient for him. Surely Allāh is to accomplish His purpose. Allāh has set a measure for everything."(65:2-3)

May Allāh ﷻ keep both of us firm on the straight path until our end (Āmīn). Always remember your father in your Duā's.

Happy Couples

Cultivate common interests
After the passion settles down, it's common to realize that you have a few interests in common. But don't minimize those activities you can do together which you both enjoy. If common interests are not present, happy couples develop them. At the same time, be sure to cultivate interests of your own as this will make you more interesting to your partner and prevent you from appearing too dependent.

Walk together
Rather than one partner lagging or dragging behind the other, happy couples walk comfortably together, side by side. They know it's more important to be with their partner than to see the sights along the way.

Make trust and forgiveness your default mode
Happy couples default to trust and forgiveness at all times. So whenever they have a disagreement they resolve it through trust and forgiveness.

Focus more on what your partner does right than what he or she does wrong
If you look for things your partner does wrong, you will always find something to blame. If you look for what he or she does right, you can always find something to appreciate. It all depends on what you want to look for. Happy couples look for the positive in each other.

Hug each other as soon as you see each other after work
Our skin has memory of "good touch" (loved), "bad touch (abused) and "no touch" (neglected). Couples who say 'As-Salāmu Alaykum' with a hug keep their skin resonated with "good touch," which will increase your spirit of love in the world.

Say "I love you" and "Inshā-Allāh, may you have a good day" every morning
This is a great way to buy some patience and tolerance as the husband sets out each day to battle traffic jams, long lines and other annoyances.

Say "As-Salāmu Alaikum" (may peace be with you) every night regardless of how you feel
This tells your partner that regardless of how upset or depressed you are, you are still happy with one another. It says that what the couple have is bigger than any single upsetting incidents.

Do a "weather" check during the day
Call your partner at home or at work to see how his or her day is going. This is a great way to adjust expectations so that you're more in synchrony of love when you connect after work. For instance, if your partner is having an awful day, it might be unreasonable to expect him or her to be enthusiastic about something good that happened to you.

Be happy to be seen with your partner
Happy couples are pleased to be seen together. Even if these actions don't come naturally, happy couples stick with each other.

How to Make Amends after a Domestic Dispute

Sayyidunā Sahl Ibn Sa'd ؓ related that the Holy Prophet ﷺ went to the house of Sayyidah Fātimah ؓ but he didn't find Sayyidunā Alī ؓ. He asked, "Where is your cousin (who was also her husband)?" She said, "There occurred between me and him something and he became angry with me so he left." The Holy Prophet ﷺ said to someone, "Find out where he is." The man said, "He is lying down in the Masjid." The Holy Prophet ﷺ went there and saw him lying down. His robe was hanging by his side and there was some dust on him. The Holy Prophet ﷺ began to say, "Stand, O' Abū Turāb; stand, O' Abū Turāb." Sayyidunā Sahl ؓ said, "He later on had no name that was more beloved to him than this name.'

When Sayyidunā Alī ؓ left the house when he became angry with his wife, it was an opportunity for him to calm his anger down that could have spun out of control had he stayed in the house, considering that she was the beloved daughter of the Noble Messenger ﷺ.

Contemplate the wisdom of the Holy Prophet ﷺ. He went over to Sayyidunā Alī ؓ in the Masjid and humorously called him Abū Turāb (the person with dust - because he was covered with dust). He was making him feel better without asking for the details or the cause of the disagreement. Sayyidah Fātimah ؓ did the same, for she did not tell her father the details of the dispute between her and her husband, 'Alī; rather, she only said, "There occurred between me and him something, he became angry with me and went outside." There is indeed an important lesson to be learned here by all husbands and wives, as well as by their parents.

Finding the Right Person to Marry

Once there was a very handsome, pious, well educated young man, whose parents encouraged him to get married. They had found so many marriage proposals but turned them all down. The parents started to suspect him of having someone else in mind. Each time the parents visited a girl's house, the young man would always say, "She's not the one!"

The young man only wanted a girl who was religious and practicing, so one evening his mother arranged for him to meet a girl who was religious and practicing.

On that evening, under supervision, the young man and girl were left to talk and ask each other questions. The young man, being a gentleman that he was, allowed the lady to ask first. The young girl asked the young man so many questions. She asked about his life, his education, his friends, his family, his habits, his hobbies, his lifestyle, his enjoyment, his pastime, his experience and even his shoe size.

The young man replied to all her questions with a smile, politely without tiring. The young girl took up all of the time (almost an hour) and thereafter asked the young man if he had any questions.

The young man said, it's ok, I only have three questions. The young girl thought, wow only three questions okay?

The young man's first question was, "Who do you love the most who's love cannot be overcome by anyone else?" She replied, this is an easy question, "My Mother."

He smiled and asked the second question, "You said that you read a lot of Qur'ān, could you tell me which Sūrahs you know the meaning of?"

Hearing this she went red and embarrassed and replied, "I do not know the meaning of any yet, but I am hoping to learn soon, Inshā-Allāh. I've just been a bit busy."

The third question the young man asked was, "I have been approached for my hand in marriage, by girls that are a lot prettier than you, why should I marry you?"

Hearing this, the young girl was outraged; she stormed off to her parents with fury, and said, "I do not want to marry this man! He is insulting my beauty and intelligence." The young man and his parent's were once again left without an agreement of marriage.

This time, the young man's parents were really angry and said, "What did you do to anger that girl? The family were so nice and pleasant and they were religious like you wanted. What did you ask the girl? Tell us!" The young man said, "Firstly I asked her, 'Who do you love the most?'" She replied, her mother.

The parents said, "So, what is wrong with that?"

The young man said, "No one is a true Muslim until he loves Allāh ﷻ and His Messenger ﷺ more than anyone else in the world."

If a woman loves Allāh ﷻ and His Messenger ﷺ more than anyone, she will love and respect me and stay faithful to me. We can then share this love, because this love is greater than lust for beauty.

The young man continued, "Then I asked, 'You read a lot of Qur'ān but can you tell me the meaning of any Sūrah?' She replied, 'No, because I haven't had time yet, so I thought of that Hadīth,

"All humans are dead except for those who have knowledge." She has lived for twenty years and not found any time to seek knowledge. Why would I marry a woman who does not know her rights and responsibilities and what will she teach my children, except how to be negligent? The woman is the Madrasah (school) and the best of teachers, and a woman who has no time for Allāh ﷻ, will not have time for her husband."

"The third question I asked her was that a lot of girls, prettier than her, had approached me for marriage, why should I choose you? That's why she stormed off, getting angry." The young man's parents responded, "It is a horrible thing to say, why would you say such a thing?! We are going back to apologise." The young man said, "I said this on purpose, to test whether she could control her anger."

When asked how to become pious, the Holy Prophet ﷺ replied, "Do not get angry, do not get angry, do not get angry, because anger is from Shaytān."

If a woman cannot control her anger with a stranger, she has just met, do you think she will be able to control it with her husband?

So, the lessons derived from this story are that marriage is based on:
Knowledge, not looks!
Practice, not preaching!
Forgiveness, not anger!
Spiritual love, not lust!
And compromise.

Search for the one... ...
Who has love for Allāh ﷻ and His Messenger ﷺ.
Who has knowledge of the Dīn and can act upon it.
Who can control their anger.
Who are willing to compromise.

The above applies to both man and a woman without exceptions.

The Holy Prophet ﷺ said, "When a man marries, he has fulfilled half of his religion, so let him fear Allāh ﷻ regarding the remaining half." (Baihaqi)

The Holy Prophet ﷺ said, "A man marries a woman for four reasons: for her wealth, for her rank, for her beauty and for her religion (and character). So marry the one who is best in religion and character and prosper."(Bukhāri, Muslim)

The Holy Prophet ﷺ said, "The most perfect believer in faith is the one whose character is finest and who is kindest to his wife."
(Tirmizi, Nasai)

The Holy Prophet ﷺ said, "A Muslim man can acquire no benefit after Islām greater than a Muslim wife who makes him happy when he looks at her, obeys him when he commands her and protects him when he is away from her in herself and in his property." (Nasai)

May Allāh ﷻ make every marriage a success, embed in us the love for Allāh ﷻ and His Messenger ﷺ and between every couple. Āmīn!

Cooking Tips

Have Wudhū whilst cooking

A person in Wudhū is safe from Shaytān (devils and evil spirits). Wudhū not only cleanses one externally but it purifies us internally by washing our sins.

Recite Sūrah Fātiha and blow over the food

Sūrah Fātiha is known as "Ruqya" (remedy) which means it can cure sickness and ward off evil.

Have the intention of cooking food solely for the pleasure of Allāh ﷻ and not for people's praises and compliments.

By doing so, the cooking will be counted as Ibādat and one will be receiving rewards. Also, if the people do not like the food then you will not feel bad because you made the food to please Allāh ﷻ, however if they do like the food, then you will receive both praises from people and the reward from Allāh ﷻ.

Keep your head & hair covered, not only to save oneself from the embarrassment of having someone pull out a hair from the food, but to keep the angels of mercy present too.

Say بِسْمِ اللهِ الرَّحْمٰنِ الرَّحِيْمِ when beginning, Allāh ﷻ will fill the food with Barakah (blessing) and Nūr (divine light).

Always check the ingredients and be conscious of Halāl and Harām. The one who consumes a single morsel of Harām food, his/her Ibādah (worship) for forty days is not accepted.

Do lots of Dhikr and recite Durūd Sharīf while cooking

The love of Allāh ﷻ and Rasūlullāh ﷺ will enter the hearts of those who eat the food.

Recite the Beautiful Names of Allāh ﷻ while cooking and it will stop arguments and fights of husband and wife and family or anyone that eats the food.

Have the pious people partake the food because the pious are the friends of Allāh ﷻ and their Duās on your behalf will be readily accepted.

Do not waste anything, not even a few grains as Allāh ﷻ hates Isrāf (wasting) and this causes reduction in the Ni'mat (favours).

When eating any food that was liked by Rasūlullāh ﷺ for example dates, meat, Tharīd, pumpkin, vinegar etc, make Niyyah (intention) of fulfilling the Sunnah to gain the rewards of following the Sunnah.

Think of yourself and the blessings of Allāh ﷻ that He is the One Who has given you the ability to cook and it is He Who puts taste in the food.

Have your servants to partake of the food too.

Say اَلْحَمْدُ لِلّٰهِ (All Praises be to Allāh) upon completing, as Allāh ﷻ made you the reason of satiating hunger and your ability to do so was from Allāh ﷻ.

Please share with the women of your homes and your friends who cook all the time. Make the whole process of cooking into an Ibādah. Inshā-Allāh.

"Who is a Man?"

Who is a Man?

A man is the most beautiful part of Allāh's ﷻ creation.
He sacrifices his chocolates for his sister.

He sacrifices his dreams for just a smile on his parents' face.

He spends his entire pocket money on buying gifts for the spouse he loves, just to see her smiling.

He sacrifices his full youth for his wife and children by working late at night without any complaint.

He builds their future by taking loans from friends and relatives repaying them for lifetime.

He struggles a lot and still has to bear scolding from his mother, wife and boss.

His life finally ends up only by compromising for others' happiness.

If he goes out, then he's careless.

If he stays at home, then he's lazy.

If he scolds his children, then he's a monster.

If he doesn't scold, then he's an irresponsible guy.

If he stops his wife from working, then he's an insecure guy.

If he doesn't stop his wife from working, then he's somebody who lives on his wife's earnings.

If he listens to mum, then he's mama's boy.

If he listens to wife, he's wife's slave.

Respect every male in your life. You will never know what he has sacrificed for you.

The Two Farewells of a Woman

Every woman is seen off from her home on two occasions. Once when she leaves her parents' home to get married, and the second time when she leaves her home in this world for her abode in the Hereafter.

Each girl grows up knowing that her parents' home is not her permanent home and that she will one day have to bid her family farewell to settle in her new home. If only all young girls would realize their second farewell as much as they do for the first farewell. Parents should mentally and physically prepare their daughters for the second departure as much as they do for the first. Although the reality is that we should prepare for the second far more than the first, for our eternal fate depends on how well we are received when we reach our final destination.

Consider the following:

During the first farewell, there is a great anxiety about whether or not the husband-to-be will be happy with her or not. In the second journey we have to worry whether or not Allāh ﷻ will be pleased with what He sees.

Before the first journey, the girl usually bathes to cleans herself, whereas for the second she will be bathed by others.

During the first journey she takes bridal goods with her, whereas the goods for the second journey is nothing but righteous deeds.

She will share her joy with every woman present at her first farewell, whereas during the second farewell she will be all alone.

During her first farewell she is dressed in the most expensive of outfits to please her husband, whereas her dress for the second journey is mere shrouds.

Invitations are handed out to celebrate the auspicious event of her wedding in this world. Allāh ﷻ Himself invites her to Jannah.

"And Allāh invites towards the abode of peace."

For her arrival, her new home in this world is decorated. For her arrival in Jannah, Allāh ﷻ decorates Jannah such that "no eye has ever seen, no ear has ever heard, nor has such beauty ever crossed anyone's imagination."

On the occasion of a wedding, the hosts welcome the guests. Imagine a celebration in Jannah, where the host is Allāh ﷻ and we are the guests! Imagine being welcomed by Allāh ﷻ, while the angels also greet us.

When we attend a wedding, we are given appetizers. When we enter Jannah each person will be given a piece of bread as an appetiser that will encapsulate all the flavours of the world.

If the husband is happy with her, the first night the woman spends with him is most cherished, and she never ever has nor will enjoy such blissful sleep as she does on the night of her wedding. Similarly, if Allāh ﷻ is happy with us when we journey to Him, the Hadīth states that the person is told in his/her grave "Sleep in the (peaceful/blissful) manner that a bride does."

If she is not accepted at her first home in the world, there is always the option of returning to the sanctuary of her parents' home where she will be taken care of. There could even be a second chance to build a new home. Whereas, if she is not accepted in the court of Allāh ﷻ in the second farewell, there is no other place of refuge and no second chance.

Ponder O' Sisters! Which farewell should we concern ourselves with more? If the journey of marriage is given so much importance, and rightly so, how much more importance should we then give to the journey of the Hereafter!

Just a Muslimah

Standing in front of the mirror,
Blinded by the sunshine,
All that can be seen is the shadow of her figure,
Her hair long and glossy,
A beautiful voluptuous body,
Causing any eye to stare unintentionally.
A figure like a trigger, she's told by many females,
In every aspect of beauty she never fails.
But as she leaves her place of sanctity,
She's covered up head to toe so modestly.
Revealing nothing but her movement,
and the sound of her footsteps.
She walks with no fear of what people might say,
as she walks forward, people move out of her way.
Men of Taqwa (piety) see her and lower their gaze,
The rest of the world is left amazed.
In summer and winter she's dressed the same,
Never abandoning her Hijāb with an excuse so lame,
All that matters to her is her Hayā (modesty) and shame.
She strives to be better each day,
Trying never to go back to her sinful ways.
She's weak, but in that weakness she expresses strength.
Allāh ﷻ is the only One she wishes to obey, She is known with
many names, Be it Ruqayyah, Ā'isha or Fātimah,
She is just a Muslimah!

By Maryum Suleman, South Africa

I Love My Husband

Mistreating someone he loves
You may not have showed good conduct or hurt someone who he loves and respects, such as his family members or close friends. Your words/actions may or may not have been intentional, but someone was hurt by it and informed your husband. Thereby causing him to be hurt and angry.

Hurt him with previous words or actions
Maybe you had said or did something quite a long time ago that really hurt him, but which he didn't mention at the time. Consequently, he had let the issue grow and took his anger randomly out on you at a later point.

Making him feel inferior
You might be a very confident and a successful person who is good at multitasking. If you are arrogant in your approach and that you are in no need of him, then this will manifest through your words/actions. You will be undermining his authority. This indicates your lack of gratefulness and recognition of his qualities and capabilities.

Committed a sin, or not doing Fardh duties

You may be committing a grave sin that your husband may or may not be aware of, but punishment is such that it can indirectly affect your marriage, particularly if a woman is unchaste. You may not be fulfilling your Farāidh e.g. Salāh, not observing proper Hijāb or engaging in un-Islamic activities, music, dance and films etc.

Socializing and going out too much

Your husband might dislike who you socialize with or that you socialize too often. He may think that you are taking advantage of his leniency or that you are never available when he wants you to be. This may result in neglecting him and your household responsibilities. Husbands have a sense of possessiveness so he might feel this is infringed if you go out so often.

Not fulfilling his desires

You may not be fulfilling his desire properly or refusing to do so altogether. This can lead to frustration and anger, as well as a cause for him to look elsewhere.

Not allowing him to spend sufficient time with his children or family

You have a problem with him spending significant amounts of time with the children or you deny him access to children (if separate), or you dislike him spending time with his own family or someone else he is close to.

These are only a few suggestions, nevertheless there are of course many more which are unique to each marriage. Wives should bear the following advice in mind when trying to resolve a problem. Understand to the best of your ability what the problem is, accept where you have gone wrong even if it may be hard to. Be sincere in pleasing Allāh ﷻ and your husband. Perform Nafl (optional Salāh) excessively, recite often and earnestly make Du'ā that Allāh ﷻ gives you patience and understanding. Pray that Allāh ﷻ reunites your hearts and brings you closer. If ones husband is still angry then, apart from seeking help, try reminding your husband of the following verses by either reciting it or placing somewhere respectable he would be able to frequently see it.

وَعَاشِرُوهُنَّ بِالْمَعْرُوفِ فَإِن كَرِهْتُمُوهُنَّ فَعَسَى أَن تَكْرَهُوا شَيْئًا وَيَجْعَلَ اللهُ فِيهِ خَيْرًا كَثِيرًا

"And live with them (women) in a beautiful manner. If then you are displeased with them (then know) perhaps you dislike something wherein Allāh has created abundant goodness in it." (4:19)

وَالْكَاظِمِينَ الْغَيْظَ وَالْعَافِينَ عَنِ النَّاسِ وَاللهُ يُحِبُّ الْمُحْسِنِينَ

"Who repress anger, who pardon people. Verily Allāh loves the good doers." (3:134)

By Sister Maryam Islām, Northampton

The Status of Women

Like a pearl, a precious gem,
given to man as a gift.

Not to be passed on in generations,
but to be loved and cared for
in those moments,
my value is more than gold,
my efforts are more, yet they seem less.

Long, loose clothes I adorn myself to cover my body,
to keep my chastity and honour my dignity,
the title of a woman I am given by the men.

I am told that I need to be liberated,
and I need to enjoy life.

My life is enjoyable, interesting and exciting,
with new experiences everyday,
and time to get closer to my Lord so I pray.

Everyday I see women on roads and in cars,
and selling themselves to men in bars,
forgetting about modesty.
Saying they're for sale,

thinking that they are successful
yet in life they fail.

Their shameless pictures on
magazine covers,
and stories about their lovers.
This is not what Islām teaches,
the status and rank of a woman,
that is what it features.

Behind every successful man is a woman,
yet their bodies they sell to the demon.
My message I wish would sail the oceans and cross the desserts:

O' Woman!!!
Keep safe your chastity and
honour your dignity,
and be like the beloved daughter of the
Holy Prophet Muhammad ﷺ,
who will be granted honour on the Day of
Judgement for her modesty.

Don't compromise your Dīn,
and your reward in Paradise will be seen!!!

By Maryum Suleman, South Africa

A Bride's Death in Sujūd

This is a true story that occurred in Abha (the capital of Asir province in Saudi Arabia).

After performing Maghrib Salāh, the new bride started preparing for her wedding ceremony by putting on her make-up and wearing her beautiful white dress. When she heard the Adhān for Ishā Salāh, she realized that she did not have Wudhū. She approached her mother and said, "Mother, I have to go to perform Wudhū and pray Ishā Salāh."

Her mother was shocked and exclaimed, "Are you crazy?! Guests are waiting to see you! What about your make up? It will be all washed away by water!!" Then she added, "I am your mother and I order you not to perform Salāh now! Wallāhi if you make Wudhū now, I will be very angry at you!"

The daughter replied, "Wallāhi I won't go out from here till I perform my Salāh! Mother you must know that there is no obedience to any creation in disobedience to the Creator!!"

Her mother said, "What will our guests say about you when you show up at your wedding ceremony without make-up?! You won't look beautiful in their eyes and they will make fun of you!"

The daughter responded with a smile, "Are you worried because I won't look beautiful in the eyes of creation? What about my Creator? I am worried because if I miss my Salāh, I won't be beautiful in His eyes?" Whilst making Wudhū, all of her make-up washed away, but she didn't care.

She started performing her Salāh until when she made Sujūd, she passed away.

Subhān-Allāh! What a great ending for this Muslimah who insisted on obeying her Lord! She put the obedience of Allāh ﷻ before anything else, so as a result, He bestowed her with an honourable ending.

She desired to be closer to Allāh ﷻ, so her wish was granted. She didn't care if she wasn't beautiful in the eyes of the creation, instead she wanted to be beautiful in the eyes of Her Creator!

O' Muslim sisters! Imagine if you were in her place! What would you do? What would you choose? Pleasing the creation or pleasing your Creator?

O' Dear sisters! Do you think you are guaranteed to live for the next minute? Next hour or even a day?

No one knows when their hour will come, nor when they will meet the Angel of Death. So ask yourselves O' sisters, how much preparations have you made for your final abode?

O' Non-Hijābi sisters! What would you choose? Pleasing others by not wearing the Hijāb or pleasing your Lord? Are you ready to meet Him without the Hijāb?

And what about you O' sisters, who are in Harām and illicit relationships? Are you ready to meet your Lord today? Tomorrow? What would you choose? Pleasures of this Dunyā or the pleasures of the Ākhirah?

May Allāh ﷻ guide us all to what pleases Him and grant everyone a good ending, Āmīn!

The Shaykh and the General

A Shaykh sits next to a general on a flight. The general asks the Shaykh: What is your occupation?

Shaykh: I'm into big business.

General: But what business exactly?
Shaykh: I deal with Allāh ﷻ.

General: Ah! So you're a religious Muslim leader? I have one problem with you Muslims, you oppress women.

Shaykh: How do we oppress women?
General: You make women cover up completely and make them generally stay in their homes.

Shaykh: Ah' I have a problem with you people, you oppress money.

General: What? How can one oppress money?

Shaykh: You keep your money hidden away, in wallets, banks and safes. You keep it covered up, why don't you display it in public if it's a beautiful thing?
General: It will get stolen obviously.

Shaykh: So you keep your money hidden because it is valuable? We value the worth of women much more. Therefore, these precious jewels are not on display to one and all. They are kept in honour and dignity.

Not for Sale for Every Male

When I look at the rose and its beauty,
I'm taken in awe by this great bounty.

Then I look around and can't help but see,
how we walk around so free.

And I don't understand my sister,
I can't comprehend.
My mind cannot fathom your beauty,
This great blessing of Allāh ﷻ, this great bounty.

Why do we let ourselves be so free?
Is our jar of confidence so empty?

Why do we let the men take advantage of you and me?
Why do we let them see?
That's what's only meant for you and me.

Do you not value your beauty?
Do you not value your chastity?
More than that of a pearl? A gem? Or a ruby..?

Are you an item on a shelf with a price tag?
That says, "I'm on for sale"
Do not let time drag!
Do you have a sticker that says,

"Made in China?" or "The United States?"

NO my sister! We are worth more!
We don't deserve to be trampled on the floor!
Don't give yourself a sticker saying "I'm on for sale!"
Rather say "I'm not for every male!"

By Maryum Suleman, South Africa

An Ideal Marriage

Hakīmul Ummah Shaykh Ashraf Alī Thānwi ﷺ once mentioned, "If I had a daughter, then whilst performing her marriage, there would be no need for a fanfare from the bridegrooms' side. I would stipulate (in writing) that he arrives with only three other attendants and brings his own clothing for the occasion. I would arrange for his stay at a nearby comfortable house. I would clothe my own daughter and not specifically invite anybody to the Nikāh. I would take everybody to the local Masjid for Salāh, after which make an announcement requesting Musallis (worshippers) to stay behind for Nikāh. I would either personally, or request an Ālim to perform the Nikāh and then distribute a small amount of dried dates. Thus, the virtues of having performed Nikāh in the Masjid would be fulfilled.

Upon arrival at home, either immediately or quite soon thereafter, I would arrange for my daughter to leave for her husband's temporary house with a reliable female aide…without any gifts. Next day, I would invite the girl back home and again, thereafter arrange for her to return. After a few days, seeing her settled, I would request the couple to depart for their home. As far as gifts are concerned, I would arrange for jewellery and property but no utensils, bed, furnishings, sweetmeats, etc. Neither would I gift anything to any relative (either side on this occasion). Yes, what I would do as long as I live, is to informally attend to their needs, when appropriate. I would purchase the property either in my own locality or their locality, and its rental income would be handed over to the couple on a regular basis with accounts."

There is much wisdom in this approach, even if it seems insignificant to some people, nevertheless is devoid of pretention and 'Riyā' (showing-off). It is designed for the couples' genuine well being, because the amount spent nowadays at engagement, weddings and honeymoon etc. is sufficient to purchase the couple's first home.

Tasbīhāt of Sayyidah Fātimah

Sayyidunā Alī once asked a student of his if he should narrate to him an incident regarding himself and Sayyidah Fātimah, the most beloved daughter of the Holy Prophet. The student replied in the affirmative.

He began, "She used to grind the mill with her own hands, which left blisters on her skin. She would sweep the house herself causing her clothes becoming dusty. Once the Messenger of Allāh received some female slaves, so I told Fātimah to go to her father and request him to give us one of them, so to help her in her work. She went to him and upon arriving in his presence, she saw a small crowd of people with him, and owing to her modesty and humility, she turned back. She felt ashamed to ask her father in front of others, so she returned home. The next day, the Messenger of Allāh came to her and asked, "Fātimah, why did you come to me yesterday?" Out of shame, she remained silent.

I explained to the Messenger of Allāh ﷺ her condition that her hands were chapped due to her grinding the mill and her chest had marks of the rope from the water-skin she would carry and also that her clothes would become dusty due to her domestic chores.

I informed the Messenger of Allāh ﷺ that I sent her to his blessed presence the previous day to ask the services of one of the slaves which he acquired.

Sayyidah Fātimah ؆ told the Holy Prophet ﷺ, "O Rasūlullāh ﷺ! Alī and I only own one bedding, which is the skin of a sheep. At night, I spread it out for us to sleep on and in the morning I place fodder and seeds in it to feed the camels."

The Holy Prophet ﷺ said, "O' my daughter, make Sabr! Prophet Mūsā ؈ had only one cloak, which he would spread as a bed at night. Aspire for Taqwa and fear Allāh ﷻ. Fulfill your duties to Allāh ﷻ and continue your household chores. When you retire to bed at night recite 33 times Subhān-Allāh, 33 times Alhamdulillāh and 34 times Allāhu Akbar. This is by far better than a slave."

Sayyidah Fātimah ؆ replied, "I am pleased with Allāh ﷻ and His Messenger ﷺ." (Abū Dāwūd)

That is whatever Allāh ﷻ and His Messenger ﷺ considered good for me, I accept wholeheartedly.

This was the life of the daughter of the king of both worlds! In the above narrated Hadīth these Tasbīhāt which are mentioned are to be read when retiring to bed at night. In other Ahādīth, it is mentioned that after every Fardh Salāh, these Tasbīhāt are to be recited 33 times each.

Recipe for a Happy Marriage

Mufti Muhammad Shāfī ؒ used to comment, "The husband/wife relationship cannot become truly prosperous until Taqwa and the fear of Allāh ﷻ doesn't become ingrained in both of their hearts." The bond between the husband and wife is so intimate that no other human relationship can be close to it. Both are each others friend.....it is impossible to even imagine a closer bond or similitude.

When both are alone and should either decide to violate, harm or forfeit the others Huqūq, then nobody can intervene. There are many rights in this world which if violated, then redress of some form is possible either through law enforcement agencies or the judiciary. However, many of the rights of marriage are such that no police officer or judge is able to enforce them. At most, they may fix maintenance to the wife; but if the husband comes home and shuns himself away, replies with sarcasm and rudeness; and creates matters whereby the wife's heart is pained, which police officer is able to charge or reform him?

The only possible remedy for such problems is the fear of Allāh ﷻ. Both need to appreciate that the others existence Allāh ﷻ has enjoined upon me and if I fail to fulfil their Haqq (right), I shall be held liable. Until this belief is not entrenched in the heart, both husband and wife are unable to truly honour each other's Huqūq.

Mufti Taqī Uthmāni Sāhib narrates,

Sometimes in order to train us, my Shaykh Dr. Abdul-Hayy Ārifī ﷺ used to comment: "We have been married fifty five years. However, Alhamdulillāh, I have never talked harshly (to my wife)."

Moreover, even his respected wife often commented: "He never ever ordered me to do anything for example, 'Fetch me some water'....or 'Do this'. I use to undertake all the tasks for him with enthusiasm and regarded it as my good fortune and honour. Nevertheless, throughout our life together he never once ordered me to do anything."

People think that walking on water or flying in the air are miracles, whereas in reality, this is a true miracle (worthy of mention). Such steadfastness is higher in rank than a thousand miracles. Over such a long period of time, undoubtedly, there must have been differences of views and disagreements....yet he never spoke to her with bitterness! Such polite behaviour is also the Sunnah of the Prophet ﷺ.

Once a person who remained a student for many years with the great Junaid Baghdadi ﷺ commented:

"Shaykh! I have not seen you performing a miracle". Junaid ﷺ replied, "O ignorant one! Have you ever observed me doing anything contrary to the Sharī'ah and Sunnah?"

Nikāh

When a man and a woman get married,
both their Īmān also get completed.
So, may your bond be strong as husband and wife,
May Allāh ﷻ grant you a happy, blissful and beautiful life.
May Allāh ﷻ fill your marriage with honesty and care,
and make sure you treat each other fair.

May your hearts be filled with everlasting love,
But ensure you always remember and obey the One above.
May you become a piece of each other's heart,
So that you miss each other when you're apart.

May you become a means of each others happiness,
And also help each other through sorrow and sadness.
May Allāh ﷻ grant you blessings in this Nikāh,
As He did to the marriages of the Holy Prophet ﷺ to Sayyidah
Khadījah ؓ and Sayyidah Āisha ؓ.
May Allāh ﷻ bless you with righteous and pious children,
Who'll become a means for you all to get united in Heaven.
But if in your marriage you face test after test,
Observe Sabr (patience) and do Shukr (gratitude)
and you'll become the best.

If either of you make a mistake,
please learn to forgive and forget,

because this is the teaching that the Holy Prophet ﷺ has set.
If ever you have any arguments,
please remember its from Shaytān,
Who'll always try to destroy one's marriage and Īmān

Always try to fulfil each other's right,
And then Inshā-Allāh the future for you will be bright.
Finally may Allāh ﷻ grant you both Jannatul-Firdaus,
And therefore grant you success,
tranquillity and happiness forever and ever.

By Muhammad Shafiq, Manchester

She Broke the Internet!

"She broke the internet" they proudly said. "Who did?" asked the little old man. Kim Kardashian broke the internet by flaunting her fully revealed, slim waistline and all the rest. We live in a world where women are awarded God-like statuses for having cheekbones so defined they can cut, for having their eyebrows finely shaped with the latest tools and for having a beautiful hourglass figure.

We live in an unfortunate society where girls know how to contour and strobe. Now don't jump the gun and box me off with the other 'Harām police' suffocating in the cabinet drawer. I am a huge lover for all things, makeup and beauty, but my concern lies when they have the power to invoke people into obsessive, obnoxious and selfish beings.

Turn on the TV, look at the billboards around you. Pick up a magazine or two, flick through your instagram and you will notice how we, as a society are dangerously fascinated, even bewitched by good looks.

This fascination is all superficial. Some may disagree and argue that this phenomenon is limited to certain groups of people or specific cultures, but I strongly believe otherwise. Being a British Asian, I have seen it on both sides and it is a topic that remains high on my 'Things I hate list'. I have witnessed women gossiping with hearts flashing in their eyes about X who is so slender, so tall and oh so rosy, in comparison to Y who, (said with almost no expression of sympathy) is on the other end of the spectrum. There will be zero recognition of piety, zero mention of intelligence and absolutely no mention of their personality. I find it incredibly sad, shallow and superficial that there are no recognition of things that actually require effort like wit, charisma, individuality, loyalty, humour, confidence, ambitious and so much more.

We are surrounded by the Kardashians who, in my personal opinion, have really escalated this vile ideology of looks over the rest.

In this difficult age, I salute women who's role models are the likes of Sayyidah Khadīja ﷺ and Sayyidah Āʾisha ﷺ. As much as I love Sayyidah Āʾisha ﷺ for her vast knowledge and defiance in the face of corruption, my heart melts with deep love for Sayyidah Khadīja ﷺ. Her existence precedes ours by over 1400 years but every aspect of her beloved personality and character can be absorbed into ours and if I can at the very least, continuously strive to mirror that, I am happy.

Sayyidah Khadīja ﷺ was the daughter of Khuwaylid and Fātima. They were almost figures of royalty amongst the Quraysh. She was widowed twice and had a son before her marriage to Prophet Muhammad ﷺ. Sayyidah Khadīja ﷺ had heard about the honesty and truthfulness of Muhammad ﷺ but asked Nafīsah and Maysarah more on his character. Why? Because ultimately that is what matters most. Muhammad ﷺ and Sayyidah Khadīja ؓ came together through character and their marriage was praised throughout Makkah.

When the Holy Prophet ﷺ would remain in Cave of Hira for days on end out of his love for isolation and contemplation, Sayyidah Khadīja ؓ never complained about his lack of given family time or his continuous absence. Rather, she, herself at the old age of fifty-five, would climb up the rocky mountain to deliver his provisions and to offer comfort.

On the day of the first revelation, when our Prophet Muhammad ﷺ descended in a state of shock and spoke those famous words asking Sayyidah Khadīja ؓ to cover him. She did not say to him that maybe you shouldn't be up there in the first place or maybe you're just going mad all alone or maybe some demons have possessed you. Instead she uttered words of comfort . She immediately tried to alleviate the grief that had struck our Prophet ﷺ by soothing him with the words that Allāh ﷻ will never disgrace you, and so on. She listed all the beautiful characteristics he possessed which in essence was telling him how much she loved him and how much Allāh ﷻ loved him.

This woman, the beautiful Sayyidah Khadīja ؓ who lived her life like a queen with all the luxuries, supported our Prophet Muhammad ﷺ with everything financially. When times got incredibly tough and the things she could not get access to that was once a basic necessity in her life, she never once wavered but defiantly stood by our Prophet Muhammad's ﷺ side with full support and loyalty.

Suddenly this support came tumbling down. Our Prophet Muhammad's ﷺ loyal wife, first believer, strong supporter, children's mother, died as a result of the boycott. She was his fallback and facilitator of his goals which she complimented.

We all need that one person who will believe in us unconditionally, who will stand by us in moments of fear, insecurity and vulnerability, who will catch us when the going gets tough, who will facilitate our ambitions and be our backbone. For our Prophet Muhammad ﷺ, Sayyidah Khadīja ؓ fulfilled all of the above.

I dream of a world where women are inspired by others other than what they are naturally blessed with. I dream of a world where every woman is more than just the fine nose and hollow cheeks. I dream of a world where every woman is driven by an inner substance and a raging ambition. I dream of a world where every woman wants to be… A KHADĪJA, NOT A KARDASHIAN!

The Etiquette of Conversing with One's Husband

Whenever the youngest wife of Sayyidunā Abū Dardā ؓ related any Ḥadīth from her husband, she would begin by saying, "My master narrated to me." The Arabic word "Sayyid" (translated as "master") is used to denote extreme respect. When the speaker attaches the word to himself/herself such as saying "Sayyidi" (my master) or "Sayyidunā" (our master), the phrase denotes love and admiration as well. When speaking with her husband, a wife should bear the following in mind:

1. She should listen attentively to what he says without speaking between his sentences. After he has spoken his piece, she may ask him something only to clarify what she does not understand. She should be silent when he is speaking because any doubts she has will most probably be explained during the course of his talk. By interrupting his speech, she may cause him to omit some important detail or to dwell on some unimportant subject.

If a wife needs to tell her husband to do something, she may tell him to do so without referring to what other men do. For example, instead of saying, "Why don't you take us out once a week like how my sister's husband does?" She should rather say, "We would really appreciate if you could take us out once a week."

2. When referring to her husband in conversations with others, a wife should not use the pronoun "he". She should refer to her hus-

band as 'my husband' or by a title people use for him. She may also refer to him as someone's father e.g. "Muhammad's father", "Zainab's father" etc.

3. A wife should always speak softly with her husband. She should never allow anger to make her raise her voice when speaking to him.

4. She should refrain from interrogating him with words like "Why?" "What?" "When?" "What for?" etc. For example, she should never question him disrespectfully by saying, "Why have you come late?" or "Why do you shout at the children?" or "What on earth did you do that for?" or "We never know where you are. Why don't you ever tell us where you are off to?"

Instead of phrasing her questions like this, she should adorn them with sweet words and gentle tones so that his heart is softened and he will respond kindly to the questions. She will then have the answers she requires without hurting her husband. For example, instead of saying, "Why have you come late?", she should say, "We waited a very long time for you to return. I cannot rest until you return. Neither the kids nor I could eat without you."

Similarly, instead of saying, "Why do you discipline the children like animals?" she should say, "You hit him very hard last night on his ear. Children sometimes lose their hearing when struck so hard. We should then not fall prey to Allāh's ﷻ wrath." She may also say, "When children are beaten, they begin to regard their parents as oppressors. They start forming the idea in their minds that their parents hit them merely to vent their anger and have no feelings for them. They convince themselves that they will be hit whether they do right or wrong. Such children then become stubborn and disobedient. We should therefore exercise patience when the children misbehave. In this way, we will be greatly rewarded. It is things like this that make parenthood a most rewarding experience. Instead of beating them, we should try to reform them in other ways. They will soon realise the error of their ways and change their habits."

Similarly, instead of rebuking him for coming late, she should say, "I would be so happy if you could inform me exactly when you expect to return so that I could prepare myself beforehand and have things ready for you." Instead of ranting and raving about being unaware of his whereabouts, she should merely express her concern for his safety, telling him that she would feel at ease if he kept her informed about where he was.

Ten Points to Maintain a Happy Marriage

Allāh ﷻ has made marriage such that it increases love between two individuals. The Holy Prophet ﷺ has said:
"We have not seen anything that creates love between two individuals such as marriage." (Ibn Mājah)

There are many ways of increasing love between the couple. Consider the following 10 points to maintain a happy marriage and control dispute.

1. Fear Allāh ﷻ: It was the noble practice of the Holy Prophet ﷺ to make the spouses aware of the fear of Allāh ﷻ before performing a Nikāh by reciting verses (An-Nisā, Al-Ahzāb, Al-Imrān) from the Holy Qur'ān. All the verses are common in the message of Taqwa (fear of Allāh ﷻ). The husband and wife will be first committed to Allāh ﷻ before being committed to each other. There can be no doubt in the success of a marriage governed by the fear of Allāh ﷻ.

2. Never be angry at the same time: Anger is the root cause for all marital disputes. One Sahābi ؓ came to the Holy Prophet ﷺ and sought some advice. The Holy Prophet ﷺ replied, "Control your anger." The same advice was rendered three times.

3. If one has to win an argument, let it be the other: The Holy Prophet ﷺ said, "Whoever discards an argument despite being correct shall earn a palace in the centre of Paradise. (Mishkāt)

4. Never shout at each other unless the house is on fire: Luqmān عليه السلام while offering advice to his son said, **"And lower your voice for verily the most disliked voice is that of a donkey." (31:19)**

5. If you have to criticize, do it lovingly: The Holy Prophet ﷺ said, "A Mu'min (believer) is a mirror for a Mu'min." (Abū Dāwūd)

6. Never bring up mistakes of the past: The Holy Prophet ﷺ said, "Whoever conceals the faults of others, Allāh ﷻ shall conceal his faults on the Day of Judgement." (Mishkāt)

7. Neglect the whole world rather than your marriage: The Holy Prophet ﷺ confirmed the advice of Sayyidunā Salmān ؓ to Sayyidunā Abū Dardā ؓ for neglecting his wife. "Verily there is a right of your wife over you." (Nasai)

8. Never sleep with an argument unsettled: Sayyidunā Abū Bakr ؓ resolved his dispute with his wife over feeding the guest before going to bed. (Bukhāri)

9. At least once everyday, express your gratitude to each other: The Holy Prophet ﷺ said, "Whoever does not show gratitude to the people, has not shown gratitude to Allāh ﷻ." (Abū Dāwūd)

10. When you have done something wrong, be ready to admit it and ask for forgiveness: The Holy Prophet ﷺ said, "All the sons of Ādam عليه السلام commit error, and the best of those who commit error are those who seek forgiveness." (Tirmizi)

Living Happily

A man and his wife were amidst a large celebration. All of their friends and family came to see the lovely ceremony and to partake of the festivities and celebrations.

A few months later, the wife came to the husband with a proposal: "I read in a book, a while ago, about how we can strengthen our marriage," she offered.

"Each of us will write a list of the things that we find a bit annoying about the other person. Then, we can talk about how we can fix them together and make our lives happier together."

The husband agreed. So each of them went to a separate room in the house and thought of the things that annoyed them about the other. They thought about this question for the rest of the day and wrote down what they came up with.
The next morning at the breakfast table, they decided that they would go over their lists.

"I'll start," offered the wife. She took out her list. It had many items on it. Enough to fill 3 pages, in fact. As she started reading the list of the little annoyances, she noticed that tears were starting to appear in her husband's eyes.
"What's wrong?" she asked. "Nothing" the husband replied, "Keep reading your list."

The wife continued to read until she had read all three pages to her husband. She neatly placed her list on the table and folded her hands over the top of it. "Now, you read your list and then we'll talk about the things on both of our lists," she said happily.

Quietly the husband said, "I don't have anything on my list. I think that in imperfections, there are adjustments. You are "perfect" the way that you are. I don't want you to change anything for me. You are lovely and wonderful and I wouldn't want to try and change anything about you."

The wife, touched by his honesty and the depth of his love for her and his acceptance of her, turned her head and wept.

In Life, there are enough times when we are disappointed, depressed and annoyed. We don't really have to go looking for them.

We have a wonderful world that is full of beauty, light and promise. Why waste time in this world looking for the bad, disappointing or annoying things when we can look around us and see the wondrous things before us?

We are happiest when we see and praise the good and try our best to forego the mistakes of our spouse. Nobody's perfect but we can find 'perfection' in them to change the way we see them. It is necessary to understand the difficulties and be a helping hand to each other that brightens up the relationship.

A Couple's Conversation

Presented here a simple conversation of a Muslim couple which never took place in reality but just in an imaginary world, but it's worth reflecting upon.

Here it begins.... Ring! Ring!

Husband: As-Salāmu Alaikum Warahmatullāhi Wabarakātuh

Wife: Wa-Alaikumus-Salām Wa-Rahmatullāhi Wabarakātuh.

Husband: How are you dear?

Wife: Looking into the mirror.....ummm... I'm pretty and fine! Alhamdulillāh. How about you?

Husband: Taking a bite of an apple.....hmm.... I'm healthy and delicious, dear. Shukr-lillāh.

Husband: Dear, are you free there?

Wife: No, I'm not.

Husband: What? What are you doing then?

Wife: Doing nothing dear.

Husband: Aren't you free then?

Wife: No, not at all.

Husband: That's really strange. What do you mean? I'm really confused.

Wife: Come on dear! Think literally. I'm not free because I'm precious and priceless.

Husband: [Burst out laughing] Dear, you are really funny and intelligent too! Māshā-Allāh! I'm really proud of you.

Wife: Thank you dear... after all whose wife am I?

Husband: Great! Well, dear I want to say to you two words right now.

Wife: Well, what are those dear?

Husband: I Love You.

Wife: Strange! Haha...aren't those three words?

Husband: No, not three, but only two.

Wife: That's amazing! Can you explain to me how?

Husband: Yes, I and You are considered as one. Aren't we?

Wife: Subhān-Allāh! You are really humorous and wise too. Māshā-Allāh! I'm really proud of you.

Husband: Thank you dear. After all, whose husband am I?

Wife: Of course mine, All praise be to Allāh Who made us each other's garments and instilled in us love and mercy.

Husband: Indeed! Glory be to him Who created us in pairs and showed us the Straight Path.

Lesson - Humour is to speech, what salt is to food and love is to the heart what blood is to the body.

Rules for a Happy Marriage

- Never be angry at the same time.
- Never yell at each other unless the house is on fire.
- If one of you has to win an argument, let it be the other one.
- If you have to criticise, do it lovingly.
- Never bring up mistakes of the past.
- Neglect the whole world rather than each other.
- Never go to sleep with an argument unsettled.
- At least once every day, try to say one kind or complimentary thing to your husband/wife.
- When you have done something wrong, be ready to admit it and ask for forgiveness. It takes two to make a quarrel.

Other titles from JKN Publications

Your Questions Answered
An outstanding book written by Shaykh Mufti Saiful Islām. A very comprehensive yet simple Fatāwa book and a source of guidance that reaches out to a wider audience i.e. the English speaking Muslims. The reader will benefit from the various answers to questions based on the Laws of Islām relating to the beliefs of Islām, knowledge, Sunnah, pillars of Islām, marriage, divorce and contemporary issues.

UK RRP: £7.50

Hadīth for Beginners
A concise Hadīth book with various Ahādeeth that relate to basic Ibādāh and moral etiquettes in Islām accessible to a wider readership. Each Hadīth has been presented with the Arabic text, its translation and commentary to enlighten the reader, its meaning and application in day-to-day life.

UK RRP: £3.00

Du'ā for Beginners
This book contains basic Du'ās which every Muslim should recite on a daily basis. Highly recommended to young children and adults studying at Islamic schools and Madrasahs so that one may cherish the beautiful treasure of supplications of our beloved Prophet ﷺ in one's daily life, which will ultimately bring peace and happiness in both worlds, Inshā-Allāh.

UK RRP: £2.00

How well do you know Islām?
An exciting educational book which contains 300 multiple questions and answers to help you increase your knowledge on Islām! Ideal for the whole family, especially children and adult students to learn new knowledge in an enjoyable way and cherish the treasures of knowledge that you will acquire from this book. A very beneficial tool for educational syllabus.

UK RRP: £3.00

Treasures of the Holy Qur'ān
This book entitled "Treasures of the Holy Qur'ān" has been compiled to create a stronger bond between the Holy Qur'ān and the readers. It mentions the different virtues of Sūrahs and verses from the Holy Qur'ān with the hope that the readers will increase their zeal and enthusiasm to recite and inculcate the teachings of the Holy Qur'ān into their daily lives.

UK RRP: £3.00

Marriage - A Complete Solution

Islām regards marriage as a great act of worship. This book has been designed to provide the fundamental teachings and guidelines of all what relates to the marital life in a simplified English language. It encapsulates in a nutshell all the marriage laws mentioned in many of the main reference books in order to facilitate their understanding and implementation.

UK RRP: £5.00

Pearls of Luqmān

This book is a comprehensive commentary of Sūrah Luqmān, written beautifully by Shaykh Mufti Saiful Islām. It offers the reader with an enquiring mind, abundance of advice, guidance, counselling and wisdom.

The reader will be enlightened by many wonderful topics and anecdotes mentioned in this book, which will create a greater understanding of the Holy Qur'ān and its wisdom. The book highlights some of the wise sayings and words of advice Luqmān ؈ gave to his son.

UK RRP: £3.00

Arabic Grammar for Beginners

This book is a study of Arabic Grammar based on the subject of Nahw (Syntax) in a simplified English format. If a student studies this book thoroughly, he/she will develop a very good foundation in this field, Inshā-Allāh. Many books have been written on this subject in various languages such as Arabic, Persian and Urdu. However, in this day and age there is a growing demand for this subject to be available in English.

UK RRP: £3.00

A Gift to My Youngsters

This treasure filled book, is a collection of Islamic stories, morals and anecdotes from the life of our beloved Prophet ﷺ, his Companions ؇ and the pious predecessors. The stories and anecdotes are based on moral and ethical values, which the reader will enjoy sharing with their peers, friends, families and loved ones.

"A Gift to My Youngsters" – is a wonderful gift presented to the readers personally, by the author himself, especially with the youngsters in mind. He has carefully selected stories and anecdotes containing beautiful morals, lessons and valuable knowledge and wisdom.

UK RRP: £5.00

Travel Companion
The beauty of this book is that it enables a person on any journey, small or distant or simply at home, to utilise their spare time to read and benefit from an exciting and vast collection of important and interesting Islamic topics and lessons. Written in simple and easy to read text, this book will immensely benefit both the newly interested person in Islām and the inquiring mind of a student expanding upon their existing knowledge. Inspiring reminders from the Holy Qur'ān and the blessed words of our beloved Prophet ﷺ beautifies each topic and will illuminate the heart of the reader.
UK RRP: £5.00

Pearls of Wisdom
Junaid Baghdādī ؓ once said, "Allāh ﷻ strengthens through these Islamic stories the hearts of His friends, as proven from the Qur'anic verse,
"And all that We narrate unto you of the stories of the Messengers, so as to strengthen through it your heart." (11:120)
Mālik Ibn Dinār ؓ stated that such stories are gifts from Paradise. He also emphasised to narrate these stories as much as possible as they are gems and it is possible that an individual might find a truly rare and invaluable gem among them.
UK RRP: £6.00

Inspirations
This book contains a compilation of selected speeches delivered by Shaykh Mufti Saiful Islām on a variety of topics such as the Holy Qur'ān, Nikāh and eating Halāl. Having previously been compiled in separate booklets, it was decided that the transcripts be gathered together in one book for the benefit of the reader. In addition to this, we have included in this book, further speeches which have not yet been printed.
UK RRP: £6.00

Gift to my Sisters
A thought provoking compilation of very interesting articles including real life stories of pious predecessors, imaginative illustrations and much more. All designed to influence and motivate mothers, sisters, wives and daughters towards an ideal Islamic lifestyle. A lifestyle referred to by our Creator, Allāh ﷻ in the Holy Qur'ān as the means to salvation and ultimate success.
UK RRP: £6.00

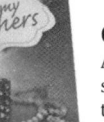

Gift to my Brothers
A thought provoking compilation of very interesting articles including real life stories of pious predecessors, imaginative illustrations, medical advices on intoxicants and rehabilitation and much more. All designed to influence and motivate fathers, brothers, husbands and sons towards an ideal Islamic lifestyle. A lifestyle referred to by our Creator, Allāh ﷻ in the Holy Qur'ān as the means to salvation and ultimate success.
UK RRP: £5.00

Heroes of Islām

"In the narratives there is certainly a lesson for people of intelligence (understanding)." (12:111)

A fine blend of Islamic personalities who have been recognised for leaving a lasting mark in the hearts and minds of people.

A distinguishing feature of this book is that the author has selected not only some of the most world and historically famous renowned scholars but also these lesser known and a few who have simply left behind a valuable piece of advice to their nearest and dearest.
UK RRP: £5.00

Ask a Mufti (3 volumes)

Muslims in every generation have confronted different kinds of challenges. Inspite of that, Islām produced such luminary Ulamā who confronted and responded to the challenges of their time to guide the Ummah to the straight path. "Ask A Mufti" is a comprehensive three volume fatwa book, based on the Hanafi School, covering a wide range of topics related to every aspect of human life such as belief, ritual worship, life after death and contemporary legal topics related to purity, commercial transaction, marriage, divorce, food, cosmetic, laws pertaining to women, Islamic medical ethics and much more.
UK RRP: £30.00

Should I Follow a Madhab?

Taqleed or following one of the four legal schools is not a new phenomenon. Historically, scholars of great calibre and luminaries, each one being a specialist in his own right, were known to have adhered to one of the four legal schools. It is only in the previous century that a minority group emerged advocating a severe ban on following one of the four major schools.

This book endeavours to address the topic of Taqleed and elucidates its importance and necessity in this day and age. It will also, by the Divine Will of Allāh ﷻ dispel some of the confusion surrounding this topic.
UK RRP: £5.00

Advice for the Students of Knowledge

Allāh ﷻ describes divine knowledge in the Holy Qur'ān as a 'Light'. Amongst the qualities of light are purity and guidance. The Holy Prophet ﷺ has clearly explained this concept in many blessed Ahādeeth and has also taught us many supplications in which we ask for beneficial knowledge.

This book is a golden tool for every sincere student of knowledge wishing to mould his/her character and engrain those correct qualities in order to be worthy of receiving the great gift of Ilm from Allāh ﷻ.
UK RRP: £3.00

Stories for Children

"Stories for Children" - is a wonderful gift presented to the readers personally by the author himself, especially with the young children in mind. The stories are based on moral and ethical values, which the reader will enjoy sharing with their peers, friends, families and loved ones. The aim is to present to the children stories and incidents which contain moral lessons, in order to reform and correct their lives, according to the Holy Qur'ān and Sunnah.
UK RRP: £5.00

Pearls from My Shaykh

This book contains a collection of pearls and inspirational accounts of the Holy Prophet ﷺ, his noble Companions, pious predecessors and some personal accounts and sayings of our well-known contemporary scholar and spiritual guide, Shaykh Mufti Saiful Islām Sāhib. Each anecdote and narrative of the pious predecessors have been written in the way that was narrated by Mufti Saiful Islām Sāhib in his discourses, drawing the specific lessons he intended from telling the story. The accounts from the life of the Shaykh has been compiled by a particular student based on their own experience and personal observation. **UK RRP: £5.00**

Paradise & Hell

This book is a collection of detailed explanation of Paradise and Hell including the state and conditions of its inhabitants. All the details have been taken from various reliable sources. The purpose of its compilation is for the reader to contemplate and appreciate the innumerable favours, rewards, comfort and unlimited luxuries of Paradise and at the same time take heed from the punishment of Hell. Shaykh Mufti Saiful Islām Sāhib has presented this book in a unique format by including the Tafseer and virtues of Sūrah Ar-Rahmān. **UK RRP: £5.00**

Prayers for Forgiveness

Prayers for Forgiveness' is a short compilation of Du'ās in Arabic with English translation and transliteration. This book can be studied after 'Du'ā for Beginners' or as a separate book. It includes twenty more Du'ās which have not been mentioned in the previous Du'ā book. It also includes a section of Du'ās from the Holy Qur'ān and a section from the Ahādeeth. The book concludes with a section mentioning the Ninety-Nine Names of Allāh ﷻ with its translation and transliteration. **UK RRP: £3.00**

Scattered Pearls

This book is a collection of scattered pearls taken from books, magazines, emails and WhatsApp messages. These pearls will hopefully increase our knowledge, wisdom and make us realise the purpose of life. In this book, Mufti Sāhib has included messages sent to him from scholars, friends and colleagues which will be beneficial and interesting for our readers Inshā-Allāh. **UK RRP: £4.00**

Poems of Wisdom

This book is a collection of poems from those who contributed to the Al-Mumin Magazine in the poems section. The Hadīth mentions "Indeed some form of poems are full of wisdom." The themes of each poem vary between wittiness, thought provocation, moral lessons, emotional to name but a few. The readers will benefit from this immensely and make them ponder over the outlook of life in general.

UK RRP: £4.00

Horrors of Judgement Day
This book is a detailed and informative commentary of the first three Sūrahs of the last Juz namely; Sūrah Naba, Sūrah Nāzi'āt and Sūrah Abasa. These Sūrahs vividly depict the horrific events and scenes of the Great Day in order to warn mankind the end of this world. These Sūrahs are an essential reminder for us all to instil the fear and concern of the Day of Judgement and to detach ourselves from the worldly pleasures. Reading this book allows us to attain the true realization of this world and provides essential advices of how to gain eternal salvation in the Hereafter.
RRP: £5:00

Spiritual Heart
It is necessary that Muslims always strive to better themselves at all times and to free themselves from the destructive maladies. This book focusses on three main spiritual maladies; pride, anger and evil gazes. It explains its root causes and offers some spiritual cures. Many examples from the lives of the pious predecessors are used for inspiration and encouragement for controlling the above three maladies. It is hoped that the purification process of the heart becomes easy once the underlying roots of the above maladies are clearly understood.   **UK RRP: £5:00**

Hajj & Umrah for Beginners
This book is a step by step guide on Hajj and Umrah for absolute beginners. Many other additional important rulings (Masāil) have been included that will Insha-Allāh prove very useful for our readers. The book also includes some etiquettes of visiting (Ziyārat) of the Holy Prophet's ﷺ blessed Masjid and his Holy Grave.
UK RRP £3:00

Advice for the Spiritual Travellers
This book contains essential guidelines for a spiritual Murīd to gain some familiarity of the science of Tasawwuf. It explains the meaning and aims of Tasawwuf, some understanding around the concept of the soul, and general guidelines for a spiritual Murīd. This is highly recommended book and it is hoped that it gains wider readership among those Murīds who are basically new to the science of Tasawwuf.
UK RRP £3:00

Don't Worry Be Happy
This book is a compilation of sayings and earnest pieces of advice that have been gathered directly from my respected teacher Shaykh Mufti Saiful Islām Sāhib. The book consists of many valuable enlightenments including how to deal with challenges of life, promoting unity, practicing good manners, being optimistic and many other valuable advices. Our respected Shaykh has gathered this Naseehah from meditating, contemplating, analysing and searching for the gems within Qur'anic verses, Ahādeeth and teachings of our Pious Predecessors. **UK RRP £1:00**

Kanzul Bāri

Kanzul Bāri provides a detailed commentary of the Ahādeeth contained in Saheeh al-Bukhāri. The commentary includes Imām Bukhāri's ﷺ biography, the status of his book, spiritual advice, inspirational accounts along with academic discussions related to Fiqh, its application and differences of opinion. Moreover, it answers objections arising in one's mind about certain Ahādeeth. Inquisitive students of Hadīth will find this commentary a very useful reference book in the final year of their Ālim course for gaining a deeper understanding of the science of Hadīth. **UK RRP: £15.00**

How to Become a Friend of Allāh ﷺ

The friends of Allāh ﷺ have been described in detail in the Holy Qur'ān and ĀHadīth. This book endeavours its readers to help create a bond with Allāh ﷺ in attaining His friendship as He is the sole Creator of all material and immaterial things. It is only through Allāh's ﷺ friendship, an individual will achieve happiness in this life and the Hereafter, hence eliminate worries, sadness, depression, anxiety and misery of this world. **UK RRP: £3.00**

Gems & Jewels

This book contains a selection of articles which have been gathered for the benefit of the readers covering a variety of topics on various aspects of daily life. It offers precious advice and anecdotes that contain moral lessons. The advice captivates its readers and will extend the narrowness of their thoughts to deep reflection, wisdom and appreciation of the purpose of our existence.
UK RRP: £4.00

End of Time

This book is a comprehensive explanation of the three Sūrahs of Juzz Amma; Sūrah Takweer, Sūrah Infitār and Sūrah Mutaffifeen. This book is a continuation from the previous book of the same author, 'Horrors of Judgement Day'. The three Sūrahs vividly sketch out the scene of the Day of Judgement and describe the state of both the inmates of Jannah and Jahannam. Mufti Saiful Islām Sāhib provides an easy but comprehensive commentary of the three Sūrahs facilitating its understanding for the readers whilst capturing the horrific scene of the ending of the world and the conditions of mankind on that horrific Day. **UK RRP: £5.00**

Andalus (modern day Spain), the long lost history, was once a country that produced many great calibre of Muslim scholars comprising of Mufassirūn, Muhaddithūn, Fuqahā, judges, scientists, philosophers, surgeons, to name but a few. The Muslims conquered Andalus in 711 AD and ruled over it for eight-hundred years. This was known as the era of Muslim glory. Many non-Muslim Europeans during that time travelled to Spain to study under Muslim scholars. The remanences of the Muslim rule in Spain are manifested through their universities, magnificent palaces and Masājid carved with Arabic writings, standing even until today. In this book, Shaykh Mufti Saiful Islām shares some of his valuable experiences he witnessed during his journey to Spain. **UK RRP: £3.00**

Ideal Youth
This book contains articles gathered from various social media avenues; magazines, emails, WhatsApp and telegram messages that provide useful tips of advice for those who have the zeal to learn and consider changing their negative habits and behavior and become better Muslims to set a positive trend for the next generation. **UK RRP:£4:00**

Ideal Teacher
This book contains abundance of precious advices for the Ulamā who are in the teaching profession. It serves to present Islamic ethical principles of teaching and to remind every teacher of their moral duties towards their students. This book will Inshā-Allāh prove to be beneficial for newly graduates and scholars wanting to utilize their knowledge through teaching. **UK RRP:£4:00**

Ideal Student
This book is a guide for all students of knowledge in achieving the excellent qualities of becoming an ideal student. It contains precious advices, anecdotes of our pious predecessors and tips in developing good morals as a student. Good morals is vital for seeking knowledge. A must for all students if they want to develop their Islamic Knowledge. **UK RRP:£4:00**